GALE

CENGAGE Learning

Drama for Students, Volume 2

STAFF

David Galens and Lynn M. Spampinato, *Editors*

Thomas Allbaugh, Craig Bentley, Terry Browne, Christopher Busiel, Stephen Coy, L. M. Domina, John Fiero, Carol L. Hamilton, Erika Kreger, Jennifer Lewin, Sheri Metzger, Daniel Moran, Terry Nienhuis, Bonnie Russell, Arnold Schmidt, William Wiles, Joanne Woolway, *Contributing Writers*

Elizabeth Cranston, Kathleen J. Edgar, Joshua Kondek, Marie Lazzari, Tom Ligotti, Marie Napierkowski, Scot Peacock, Mary Ruby, Diane Telgen, Patti Tippett, Kathleen Wilson, Pam Zuber, *Contributing Editors*

Pamela Wilwerth Aue, *Managing Editor*

Jeffery Chapman, *Programmer/Analyst*

Victoria B. Cariappa, *Research Team Manager*
Michele P. LaMeau, Andy Guy Malonis, Barb

McNeil, Gary Oudersluys, Maureen Richards, *Research Specialists*

Julia C. Daniel, Tamara C. Nott, Tracie A. Richardson, Cheryl L. Warnock, *Research Associates*

Susan M. Trosky, *Permissions Manager*
Kimberly F. Smilay, *Permissions Specialist*
Sarah Chesney, *Permissions Associate*
Steve Cusack, Kelly A. Quin, *Permissions Assistants*

Mary Beth Trimper, *Production Director*
Evi Seoud, *Assistant Production Manager*
Shanna Heilveil, *Production Assistant*

Randy Bassett, *Image Database Supervisor*
Mikal Ansari, Robert Duncan, *Imaging Specialists*
Pamela A. Reed, *Photography Coordinator*

Cynthia Baldwin, *Product Design Manager*
Cover design: Michelle DiMercurio, *Art Director*
Page design: Pamela A. E. Galbreath, *Senior Art Director*

ISSN applied for and pending
Printed in the United States of America
10 9 8 7 6 5 4 3

Glengarry Glen Ross

David Mamet

1983

Introduction

David Mamet's *Glengarry Glen Ross* was first
presented at the small Cottlesloe Theatre of the
Royal National Theatre, in London, England, on
September 21, 1983. The critics gave the play
strongly positive reviews and the production played
to sold-out audiences. It was later awarded the
Society of West End Theatres Award (similar to the
American "Tony" Award) as best new play. The
American premier of *Glengarry Glen Ross* took

place at Chicago's Goodman Theatre on February 6, 1984; with one cast change, the production then transferred to Broadway's Golden Theatre on March 25. With very few exceptions, the New York critics recognized the play as brilliant in itself and a major advance for Mamet as a playwright. Nevertheless, ticket sales were slow and the play lost money for two weeks. After it was awarded the Pulitzer Prize, sales increased significantly. It ultimately ran for 378 performances, closing on February 17, 1985.

Many critics in both England and America pointed out that, for all its use of "four-letter words," *Glengarry Glen Ross* is a morality play. They noted that the work is an abrasive attack on American business and culture and a withering depiction of the men whose lives and values are twisted by a world in which they must lie, cheat, and even steal in order to survive. Virtually all of the critics commented extensively on Mamet's use of language, not only to create tension and define character, but also as a sort of musical poetry: "hot jazz and wounding blues," as Frank Rich, critic for the *New York Times* put it. Even those few critics who were lukewarm about the play as a whole appreciated the distinctive, powerful language. Critics also appreciated the savage, scalding comedy of the play.

The influences of playwrights Samuel Beckett and Harold Pinter on Mamet has been pointed out by numerous critics, and Mamet has said that he has also been influenced by Lanford Wilson, Eugene

Ionesco, Bertolt Brecht, and Anton Chekhov. He has also acknowledged the influence of Thorstein Veblen's *Theory of the Leisure Class*. A strong nonliterary influence has been his study of the Stanislavsky system (named for the famed director of the Moscow Art Theatre, Konstantin Stanislavsky) of actor training as interpreted and taught by Sanford Meisner and Lee Strasberg at the Actors Studio.

Author Biography

David Mamet was born in Chicago, Illinois, on November 30, 1947. His father was a labor lawyer and his mother a schoolteacher. After his parents' divorce in 1958, Mamet lived with his mother and sister. He played football, wrestled, and was a voracious reader. In 1963, he moved to North Chicago to live with his father and attend the private Francis Parker school where he first took drama classes and played the lead in a musical. He also worked backstage at Hull House theatre and at the famous improvisational Second City Company.

Mamet studied literature and drama at Goddard College in Vermont, where he received a B.A. degree in 1969. His first short play, *Camel,* was written to fulfill his thesis requirement. During his time at Goddard, he spent a year "in the field" at the Neighborhood Playhouse School of the Theatre in New York City, where he studied the Stanislavsky system of acting under the direction of Sanford Meisner. During his college years Mamet's summer jobs included work as an actor and "specialty dancer" with several theatres. Following his graduation in 1969, he worked in Montreal with a company based on the campus of McGill University. He then returned to Chicago where he worked as a cab driver and, for almost a year, in the office of a "dubious" real estate firm. The latter experience is clearly evident in *Glengarry Glen Ross.* In 1970, Mamet taught acting at Marlboro

College in Vermont, where he wrote *Lifeboat,* based on his experiences with one summer job. The following two years, he taught at Goddard and, while there, presented the first versions of *Duck Variations* and *Sexual Perversity in Chicago. Duck Variations* was subsequently presented in Chicago in the fall of 1972, marking the first production of a play by Mamet in his hometown. In the fall of 1973, Mamet moved back to Chicago. *Sexual Perversity in Chicago* was presented by the Organic Theatre Company in the summer of 1974, drew large audiences, and was awarded the prestigious Joseph Jefferson Award. In 1975 he completed *American Buffalo* and that work was presented by the Goodman Theatre with critical and popular success. On January 23, 1976, *American Buffalo,* with a new cast, opened at St. Clement's theatre in New York City, receiving generally positive notices. Mamet moved to New York the next month. That summer *Sexual Perversity in Chicago* and *Duck Variations* opened at the Off-Broadway Cherry Lane Theatre, where they would enjoy a long run; in February 1977, *American Buffalo* opened on Broadway and was awarded the New York Drama Critics' Circle Award.

Mamet's career flourished throughout the 1980s and 1990s, with such notable works as *Edmund* (1982), *Glengarry Glen Ross* (1983), *Speed-the-Plow* (1988), and *Oleanna* (1992). He also ventured into film during this period, writing the scripts for *The Postman Always Rings Twice* (1981), *The Verdict* (1982)—which won an Academy Award nomination—*The Untouchables*

(1987), and *Hoffa* (1992). His success as a screenwriter led to opportunities as a director, including the films *House of Games* (1988), *Homicide* (1991), and *Oleanna* (1995), all of which he also wrote.

Plot Summary

Act I

Glengarry Glen Ross has a daring structure with two very different forms for the two acts. Act One is broken up into three scenes, each set in a different booth in a Chinese restaurant in Chicago; while not clearly stated, all of the action may be occurring simultaneously. Through these scenes we come to know the jargon of the real estate sales world: "lead" is a sales prospect; the "board" is a chart of sales closings; "sit" is a face-to-face meeting with a prospect; "closing" is getting the customer's signature on a contract and a check. We also learn, bit by bit, that there is a sales contest on and that the winner of the first prize will receive a Cadillac, second prize a set of steak knives—all the rest of the salesmen will be fired.

In the first scene, Shelly Levene, once a top salesman but now, in his fifties, down on his luck, is begging Williamson, the real estate office manager, for "A-list" leads. Levene has not closed a sale in months—but he is convinced that one good lead will restore his confidence and put him back on track. As the salesman becomes more desperate, Williams offers to sell him the leads for $50 each—and a percentage of any commissions Levene might earn. Levene agrees to the offer but doesn't have the cash.

In the second scene, David Moss and the hopeless George Aaranow, both men in their fifties, commiserate about the difficulties of closing a sale, especially without the good leads—and the good leads go only to those who close sales. Moss suggests that if they could steal the leads from their office a competitor would be willing to buy them. When Aaranow asks if Moss is suggesting a burglary, Moss acts as if the thought had never occurred to him. However, he eventually not only suggests a burglary but insists that Aaranow must carry it out and that Aaranow is already involved as an "accessory" before the fact "because you listened."

In the third scene, Richard Roma, the office's star salesman, is talking with a man named Jim Lingk. Roma delivers a virtual monologue that seems to be about sex, loneliness, and the vagaries and insecurities of life. His tone is intimate and conversational, indicating that Lingk is an old friend of his. At the end, however, his tone changes and it is revealed that he has been lulling Lingk into a sales pitch with his casual demeanor.

Act II

Act II plays out the forces set in motion in the previous act with a more conventional structure. It is also much more comic than the first act. The act opens in the ransacked real estate office the next morning. A police detective, Baylen, is there to investigate the burglary and one by one the salesmen are called into Williamson's office to talk to the detective. Roma arrives and demands to know if his contract for the sale of land to Lingk the previous night had been filed or stolen. Williamson waffles but eventually says that it was filed before the burglary. The sale will put Roma "over the top" and win him the Cadillac. Aaranow is nervous about being questioned and Roma advises,"tell the truth, George. Always tell the truth. It's the easiest thing to remember." Levene enters and says he has just sold eight parcels (properties). As he is discussing the closing, Moss comes out of the office highly insulted by Baylen's accusatory treatment. The tension leads to savage, and very funny, confrontations with Roma and Levene. After Moss stalks out, Levene continues crowing about his success with Roma flattering and egging him on. Williamson comes in and Levene boasts about his sale. He attacks the office manager, telling him he has no "balls" and belittling him for having never been out on a sit. Roma spots Lingk coming into the building and smells trouble. He and Levene quickly go into an improvised scene with Levene playing a rich investor. Lingk is there because his wife insisted he cancel the contract. Roma stalls him saying that he has to get Levene to the airport. He further states that he has a prior obligation and that he will talk to Lingk on the following Monday. Lingk says that he has to cancel before that—his wife has called the Attorney General's office and the contract cannot go into effect for three business days after the check has been cashed. Roma claims that the check hasn't been cashed and that it won't be cashed until after he has talked to Lingk the following Monday. Aaranow bursts into the middle of this scene complaining about how he was treated by Baylen. Williamson, trying to be helpful, tells Lingk that his check has already been cashed. Lingk leaves after apologizing profoundly to Roma for having to back out of the deal. Roma screams at Williamson for ruining his deal. Seething, he goes into the office for his interrogation with the detective. Levene picks up where Roma left off, attacking Williamson for scuttling his friend's sale. In his anger, Levene lets slip that he knew the contract had not in fact gone to the bank. Williamson realizes that the only way Levene could have known this information was if he had been in the office the night before, which he states. Williamson now knows that it was Levene who broke into the office and stole the leads. Adding insult to the broken salesman's injury, he also points out that Levene's sale was worthless—the people he closed were well-known eccentrics who had no money. When Roma comes back, Williamson enters his office to talk with Baylen. Roma says he wants to form a partnership with Levene. When Levene goes in to talk with Baylen, Roma tells Williamson that his "partnership" with Levene means that Roma gets all of his own commission and half of Levene's. The play ends with Aaranow saying that he hates his job and Roma leaving for the Chinese restaurant to hunt for more prospects.

George Aaranow

George Aaranow is a fairly stupid salesman in his fifties who seems to be sucked into Moss's scheme to steal the leads and sell them to a competitor. In Act II, Aaranow displays the only loyalty shown in the play: he keeps his mouth shut about Moss.

Baylen

Baylen is a police detective in his early forties. He is in the ransacked office in Act II to investigate the burglary and, although we never see him in direct questioning, he is rough enough to outrage even the tough salesmen.

Shelly Levene

Shelly Levene is a man in his fifties, formerly a hot salesman and now down on his luck. He needs a sale to survive. In Act I, scene 1, Levene pleads with his office manager, Williamson, for good leads and agrees to bribe him but doesn't have the necessary cash. Levene is so strapped for cash that he even has to worry about having enough to buy gas. He is the only character about whom we learn anything of his outside life: he lives in a resident hotel, he has a daughter, and the daughter is apparently dependent on him and perhaps is even in a hospital. When we see him in Act II, he enters the ransacked office crowing about having just closed a sale for eight parcels. He tells a detailed story of how he forced the buyers, two old people with little money, to close. In his new-found glory, he also berates Williamson for not being a man, for not knowing how to sell. In his excitement, he lets slip the fact that he knew that Williamson had not turned in Roma's contract for the Lingk sale the night before and Williamson perceives that Levene could know that only if he had been in the office. He knows that Levene did the burglary and, in spite of pleading by Levene, turns him in to the police.

Media Adaptations

- *Glengarry Glen Ross* was adapted as a film by David Mamet, directed by James Foley, and starring Jack

Lemmon, Al Pacino, Ed Harris, Alec Baldwin, Alan Arkin, Kevin Spacey, Jonathan Pryce, Bruce Altman, and Jude Ciccolella; distributed by LIVE Entertainment, Movies Unlimited, Baker & Taylor Video.

James Lingk

James Lingk is a customer to whom Roma sells a parcel of land. Lingk's wife sends him back to cancel the deal, thus leading to an impromptu improvisational scene between Roma and Levene and a blown deal because of Williamson's intrusion. Even after he knows that Roma lied to him, Lingk apologizes for breaking the deal.

The Machine

See Shelly Levene

Dave Moss

Dave Moss is a bitter man in his fifties who sets up a deal to sell the stolen leads to a competing firm headed by Jerry Graff. In Act I, scene 2, he seems to have trapped George Aaranow, a fellow salesman, into doing the actual burglary. In Act II we see an outraged Moss after he has been interrogated by the police. He says that no one should be treated that way and decides to leave for the day. Later, in an attempt to save himself, Levene tells Williamson that it was Moss who set up the burglary.

Richard Roma

Richard Roma, in his early forties, is the "star" salesman of the office. In Act I, scene 3, he seems to be talking to a friend but it turns out that he is merely softening up a stranger, Jim Lingk, for a sales pitch. In Act II we learn that he did close the deal but sees the deal fall through due to the ignorant intrusion of Williamson. Near the end of the play Roma seems to want to team up with Levene but even that apparent show of unity is just another scam.

John Williamson

John Williamson, a man in his early forties, is the office manager and is in charge of giving the "leads" to the salesmen. This gives him great power. He gives the best leads to those who have the best sales records, and the only way to sell is to have the best leads. In Act I he agrees to give top leads to Levene if Levene pays him fifty dollars per lead and twenty percent of his commissions. In Act II, Williamson is with the police detective, Baylen, questioning the salesmen. Williamson does intrude into the scene being played out by Roma and Levene in an attempt to keep Lingk from cancelling his contract and, in his ignorance, manages to spoil the deal. Both Roma and Levene attack him verbally and Levene lets slip the clue that allows Williamson to expose Levene as the burglar.

Themes

The plot of *Glengarry Glen Ross* is simple: in Act I in three brief two-person scenes set in a Chinese restaurant we meet the principal characters and learn that they are under extreme pressure to sell apparently worthless land in Florida and that to succeed in this they need good sales "leads," which are under the control of the reptilian office manager, Williamson. Act II begins the next morning; the office has been ransacked and the leads stolen. The act ends with the apprehension of Levene, one of the salesmen, as the thief.

Topics for Further Study

- Read *The Death of a Salesman* by Arthur Miller and compare the view of selling in that play with that in

Glengarry Glen Ross. Is Willy Loman anything like the salesmen in *Glengarry Glen Ross?*

- Investigate consumer protection laws in your state. Do you think they are needed to protect the consumer, or do they just provide more red tape for the businessperson?

- Explore environmental problems caused by overdevelopment in Florida, Arizona, or Southern California.

- How much does the name of a product reflect what that product actually is rather than what the producer would like us to think it is?

- Are there limits on capitalism now? If so, what are they? Should there be more or fewer?

Duty and Responsibility

The major theme of *Glengarry Glen Ross* is business and, by extension, capitalism. Mamet never discusses, neither to praise nor to condemn, the workings of business; he shows the quintessential paradigm of business, the salesman, striving to survive by his wits in the system and how it damages and drains his better humanity. In the published play, Mamet includes a quote of the

"Practical Sales Maxim: 'Always Be Closing.'"
Everything is business, even personal relationships.

American Dream

The American dream that we can "get ahead" through honest hard work is undermined by the fact that, for these salesmen at least, the only measure of success is material and the only way to succeed is to sell. They are selling land—probably worthless land —to people who dream that buying that land will somehow provide the big score, the chance to make large profits when they resell it. It is interesting to note that no one mentions building on or settling on the land; it is always referred to as an investment opportunity. Moreover, the salesmen will say anything and promise anything to "close."

Alienation and Loneliness

Certainly all of the characters suffer alienation both from nature and other people. They are apparently unfamiliar with the land they sell and refer to it as "crap." It is just a commodity. They are also alienated from their customers, whom they despise, and from each other. They do have a unity in despising what they know is an unfair system, but whenever it seems that friendship is involved— whether with one another or with a customer—we soon learn that it is just another scam, another preparation for "closing." For example, Moss seems to commiserate with Aaranow but is really setting him up to do a burglary for him; Roma seems to be having a heartfelt conversation with Lingk, and it even appears to the audience that they are old friends; but, we find that he is just disarming a stranger when he produces a sales pamphlet; Roma suggests that he and Levene work as partners only to betray him almost immediately afterwards.

Language

Language will be discussed in some detail under "style," but it should be noted here that language is also a major theme in *Glengarry Glen Ross*. Language as a means of communication has been subverted. Nothing that is said is necessarily true even when it seems to be in support of friendship or to express a philosophy of life. Language is used by these people solely as a tool to manipulate potential customers and each other.

Deception

Deception is at work on every level. We see lying and fantasy as a way of thinking and operating: certainly there seems to be little truth to anything anyone says to anybody. The most explicit example is in Act II when Lingk comes to the office to cancel his contract. Roma and Levene put on an elaborate improvised show for him in which Levene pretends to be an important executive with American Express who is a large investor in the land Roma is trying to sell. Throughout the play, the characters immediately turn to deception when they are in a tight corner—which is most of the time.

Success and Failure

Success and failure are very easily measured in the closed world of *Glengarry Glenn Ross* and by extension in the larger world of American capitalism. To succeed is to get money; to fail is not to get money. Again, it is not only the salesmen who measure success materially: their customers also think that if they buy the land they will sell it at a huge profit and eventually get something for nothing. Also, if these people do not make sales their whole sense of self is destroyed. For the salesman, selling is not just a job but a persona; it is who and what they are.

Morals and Morality

There is no mention of morals or morality or even business ethics in *Glengarry Glen Ross*. Morality and ethics are not part of the operating procedure. In Roma's pseudo-philosophical discourse to Lingk, he says that he does "that today which seem to me correct today." While Roma purports to accept that there may be an absolute morality, he says, "And then what?" It is the very absence of morality which gradually dawns on the audience and frames the entire play. These people operate in a vicious jungle in which only the strong survive and nothing else matters.

Conscience

Similarly, not one of the characters is troubled

by conscience. Conscience does not seem to exist as a part of anyone's makeup. Again, it is Roma who mentions the concept in Act I, scene 3: "You think that you're a thief? So What? You get befuddled by a middle-class morality . . . ? Get shut of it. Shut it out. You cheated on your wife . . .? You did it, live with it. (Pause) You fuck little girls, so be it?"

Sexism

Glengarry Glen Ross depicts a world of men and men's relationships. Selling is the sign of manhood. Roma and Levene both tell Williamson that he is not a man because he has never actively made sales. There are only two females who are even mentioned in the play: Lingk's wife and Levene's daughter. Lingk's wife has forced Lingk to confront Roma and cancel his contract. Roma commiserates with him and, seemingly at least, wants to talk to him man-to-man about his problems. Lingk does cancel the contract with apologies for having "betrayed" Roma. Levene's daughter, for whom he has provided an education, is apparently ill. This barely-mentioned daughter seems to provide the only glimpse of human warmth in this group of men.

Anger and Hatred

In that world of vicious competition devoid of morality or friendship, all the characters seem to operate out of anger and hatred: they are angry at Williamson for not producing better leads; they are angry with each other because the success of one means the failure of another. They are caught in an unfair system and they know it. Finally, at the end of the play, Aaranow states openly what all, with the possible exception of Roma, feel: "Oh, God, I hate this job."

Plot

The structure of *Glengarry Glen Ross* is unusual. Act I consists of three brief scenes, each scene a duologue. Through these scenes we learn the jargon of the real estate sales world, come to know the characters involved, and are introduced to the possiblity of a burglary of the sales office by two of the salesmen. Act II has a more conventional structure and is similar to that of a mystery play in which the perpetration of the crime is sought and caught. However, it would be a mistake to think that the interest of *Glengarry Glen Ross* is sustained by the plot. The main action is contained in the language and takes place through the shifting relationships and stories of the characters.

Action

Mamet is very clear about what is important in his plays. In one of his essays in *Writing in Restaurants* he points out that it is not the theme of the play to which we respond, but the action. In another essay in the same book he points out that "good drama has no stage directions. It is the interaction of the characters' objectives expressed solely by what they say to each other—not by what the author says about them." There is very little description even of the set in *Glengarry Glen Ross* and no directions for character action. Character is habitual action, and the author shows us what the characters do. It is all contained in the dialogue. There is no nonessential prose.

Language

In *Writing in Restaurants* Mamet says, "Technique is knowledge of how to translate incohate desire into clear action—into action capable of communicating itself to the audience." The Characters in *Glengarry Glen Ross* are created by the language they use and, for the salesmen, at least, their livelihoods depend on their use of language. This language is not used to communicate truth but rather to hide truth, to manipulate others, savagely attack each other, and to tell stories that celebrate victory—as Levine does when telling how he closed a deal for eight parcels of land. It is no mistake that the salesmen far outshine the office manager Williamson, the customer Lingk, and the police detective Baylen (although through the reactions of Aaranow and Moss we know that Baylen also uses language powerfully when he is in charge of the interrogation off stage in Williamson's office.) Language is ammunition in the primal battles for power and survival.

It is widely agreed that Mamet has an exact ear for male dialogue (Robert Cushman, an English critic, says, "Nobody alive writes better American"). However, his language is not naturalistic, not an exact copy of how people really declaring that his coal advisory commission was a well-balanced mix: "I have a black, a woman, two Jews, and a cripple."

In the Soviet Union, commercial fishing ceased in the Aral Sea. The draining of water from the inland sea's two source rivers in a massive project to irrigate surrounding desert had shrunk the sea by one third, doubled its salinity, and created an ecological disaster as winds blew chemically contaminated dust and salt from the sea bottom onto surrounding fields, poisoning water supplies and even mothers' milk

Communications

In December, Chicago motorists began talking on cellular telephones in their cars, available at $3,000 plus $150 per month for service. The telephones quickly became not only handy business tools but highly desirable status symbols.

Miscellaneous

Cabbage Patch dolls became black market items as stores ran out of supplies.

Critical Overview

The initial critical reactions in London to *Glengarry Glen Ross* were overwhelmingly, but not unanimously, positive. Robert Cushman in the *Observer* called it "the best play in London." He was especially taken with Mamet's use of language and mentioned his "fantastic ear for emphasis and repetition and the interrupting of people who weren't saying anything anyway. Nobody alive writes better American." He went on to say, "Here at last, carving characters and conflicts out of language, is a play with real muscle: here, after all the pieces we have half-heartedly approved because they mention 'important' issues as if mentioning were the same as dealing with. *Glengarry Glen Ross* mentions nothing, but in its depiction of a driven, consciousless world it implies a great deal."

Michael Billington in the *Guardian* talked of Mamet's brilliant use of language to depict character and attitudes and praised both the play and the production. Milton Shulman in the *Standard* praised the play and said, "There is a glib, breathtaking momentum in the speech rhythms that Mamet has devised for this pathetic flotsam." Clive Hirschhorn in the *Sunday Express* was not enthusiastic about the first act, but called the second act "a dazzler." Michael Coveny in the *Financial Times* was enthusiastic and said, "The text bubbles like a poisoned froth." Giles Gordon in the *Spectator* called the play "something of a letdown," and went on to say of the production that the "actors give the performances they always give."

In New York, the plaudits were even greater. The most important critic, Frank Rich of the *New York Times,* gave a rave review of the play and said, "This may well be the most accomplished play its author has yet given us. As Mr. Mamet's command of dialogue has now reached its most dazzling pitch, so has his mastery of theatrical form." Howard Kissel in the influential *Women's Wear Daily* was very positive and mentioned that, in spite of the lack of physical movement in the first act (which he likened to "some arcane Oriental puppet theatre"), the mood was not static: "intense animation comes from Mamet's brilliant dialogue, the vulgar sounds one hears on any street corner shaped into a jarring, mesmerizing music."

The headline above Clive Barnes's *New York Post* review read, "Mamet's 'Glengarry:' A Play To See and Cherish." Barnes called it "Mamet's most considerable play to date." He said that Mamet's language was able to "transform the recognizable into the essential," and that "the characters and situations have never looked more special." Jack Kroll in *Newsweek* said, "Mamet seems to get more original as his career develops," and called him, "The Aristophanes of the inarticulate." He went on to say, "He is that rarity, a pure writer." Dennis Cunningham of WCBS said, "I could simply rave to the heavens," and called *Glengarry Glen Ross* a "theatrical event, altogether extraordinary, an astonishing, exhilarating experience . . . and that rarest of Broadway achievements, a major American play by a major American playwright." Douglas Watt of the *Daily News* found the play dull and said, "To elevate it to the status of a bitter comment on the American dream would amount to cosmic foolishness. It is what it is, a slice of life."

Glengarry Glen Ross continues to receive serious critical attention. The first book-length study of Mamet was C. W. E. Bigsby's *David Mamet,* published in 1985, which studies Mamet's works from the beginning through *Glengarry Glen Ross.* Bigsby sees Mamet as a major writer whose concern has been with "dramatizing the inner life of the individual and of the nation." Dennis Carroll's book-length study, *David Mamet,* published in 1987, assesses Mamet at "Mid-Career," and deals with the plays in thematic categories. Carroll also considers Mamet's place in the larger context of drama and theatre and points out that, while each major play is open to many different interpretations,' "This is the mark of any major artist whose special qualities nag at the sensibilities, but who cannot be too easily pigeonholed or defined. His achievements already stamp him as a major American playwright of his generation, whose work has both the vividness and the power to cross national boundaries."

A brilliant major study by Anne Dean, *David Mamet: Language as Dramatic Action,* focuses on Mamet's celebrated use of language and Mamet as a dramatic poet. There have been many critical essays dealing with *Glengarry Glen Ross,* some of the best collected in *David Mamet: A Casebook,* edited by Leslie Kane. Mamet and *Glengarry Glen Ross* have also become the subjects of numerous masters theses and doctoral dissertations.

What Do I Read Next?

- *American Buffalo,* Mamet's 1975 play about three low-life men plotting to steal a rare coin, gives another slant on Mamet's view of American business.

- *Speed-the-Plow* is Mamet's 1987 "Hollywood play" produced in New York with Joe Mantegna, Ron Silver, and Madonna.

- *Oleanna,* Mamet's 1992 play, deals with teaching and the power of "political correctness" to utterly destroy a college professor.

- *The Death of a Salesman* is Arthur Miller's 1947 classic play about a salesman and distorted values in America.

- *Writing in Restaurants,* a book of essays by Mamet, gives a good look at his philosophy of writing and his view of contemporary America.

- *A Whore's Profession,* 1996, is Mamet's most recent book of essays about working as a writer.

- The entry on David Mamet by Patricia Lewis and Terry Browne in *Dictionary of Literary Biography,* Volume 7: *Twentieth-Century American Dramatists,* published in 1981 by Gale, gives a good overview of Mamet's early works.

Further Reading

Bigsby, C. W. E. *David Mamet,* Methuen, 1985, p. 15.

> The first book-length study of Mamet covers from the beginning through *Glengarry Glen Ross.* An excellent introduction to the approaches and themes of Mamet.

Carroll, Dennis. *David Mamet,* MacMillan, 1987, p. 155.

> An excellent assessment of Mamet at mid-career, from the beginnings through *Glengarry Glen Ross* approached by thematic groupings.

Dean, Anne. *David Mamet: Language as Dramatic Action,* Associated University Presses, 1990, pp. 96-197.

> A brilliant analysis of Mamet's use of language, approached overall and play-by-play. There are also useful insights into themes and the rehearsal process taken from interviews by the author.

Gordon, Clive. Review of *Glengarry Glen Ross* in the *Spectator,* September 27, 1983.

> A remarkably unperceptive and arrogant review of the London

production.

Kane, Leslie. Interview with Joe Mantegna, in her *David Mamet: A Casebook,* Garland, 1992, pp. 254-55, 259.

> A fascinating look into the work of a fine actor in approaching and rehearsing a character. There are other essays in the *Casebook* that are helpful, notably "Power Plays: David Mamet's Theatre of Manipulation" by Henry I. Schvey; and "Comedy and Humor in the Plays of David Mamet" by Christopher C. Hudgins.

Mamet, David. *Writing in Restaurants,* Penguin, 1986, pp. 3, 6, 13, 14, 20, 32, 116, 124-25.

> A broad range of essays that are very useful in understanding of Mamet's view of theatre, tradition, technique, and life in general.

Rich, Frank. Review of *Glengarry Glen Ross* in the *New York Times,* March 26, 1984.

> A long, rich, and insightful review of the New York production.

Sources

Barnes, Clive. Review of *Glengarry Glen Ross* in the *New York Post,* March 26, 1984.

Billington, Michael. Review of *Glengarry Glen Ross* in *Guardian,* September 25, 1983.

Coveney, Michael. Review of *Glengarry Glen Ross* in *Financial Times,* September 22, 1983.

Cushman, Robert. Review of *Glengarry Glen Ross* in *Observer,* September 25, 1983.

Hirschhorn, Clive. Review of *Glengarry Glen Ross* in *Sunday Express,* September 25, 1983.

Kissel, Howard. Review of *Glengarry Glen Ross* in *Womens Wear Daily,* March 26, 1984.

Kroll, Jack. Review of *Glengarry Glen Ross* in *Newsweek,* April 9, 1984.

Shulman, Milton. Review of *Glengarry Glen Ross* in the *Standard,* September 22, 1983.

Watt, Douglas. Review of *Glengarry Glen Ross* in the *Daily News,* March 26, 1984.

CPSIA information can be obtained
at www.ICGtesting.com
Printed in the USA
LVOW13s0833080318
569117LV00017B/420/P